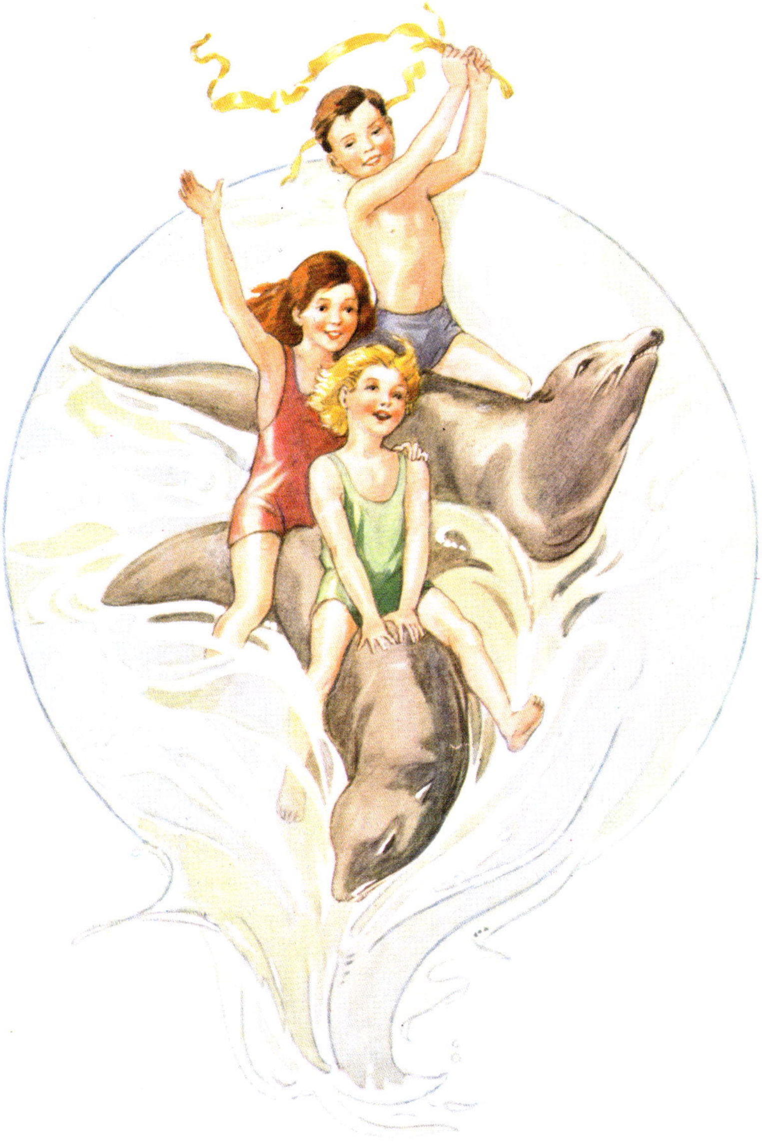

Margaret Tarrant & her pictures

by John Gurney

THE MEDICI SOCIETY LTD
LONDON

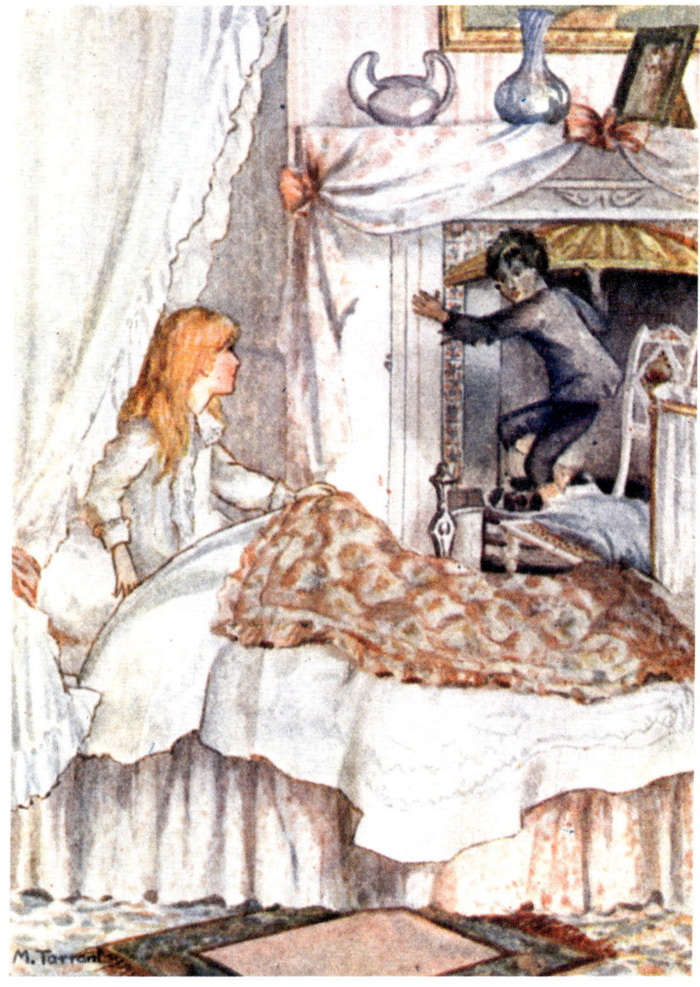

"Up jumped the little white lady." from *The Water Babies* by Charles Kingsley. J. M. Dent, 1908.

When Margaret Tarrant was just 19 she was commissioned by J.M.Dent & Sons, who published many books for children, to illustrate a new edition of Charles Kingsley's *The Water Babies,* and this was published in 1908. This had been first published in 1863 when Kingsley was Rector of Eversley in Hampshire. The story tells of how Tom the chimney sweep was sent up a large chimney by his difficult master Mr Grimes and how he lost his way in the chimney stack of the big house and came down into a lovely girl's bedroom, of how he was so upset that he escaped through the window, fell into the river, and was washed down to the sea and changed into a water baby. It recounts his exciting adventures there and how he learned to be kind to and thoughtful for others, which brought him happiness. *The Water Babies* and *Westward Ho!* by Kingsley are still much loved stories.

Many more commissions followed and for the next 12 years she concentrated on children's books. For Ward Lock & Co. she illustrated seven books including *Alice in Wonderland,* 1916, Hans Anderson's *Fairy Stories,* 1917, and *Nursery Rhymes* in 1914 and 1923. For George G. Harrap & Co. she illustrated some 20 books between 1915 and 1929 including several books by Marion St.John Webb, who also wrote fairy books including *The Magic Lamplighter* illustrated by Margaret Tarrant for the Medici Society.

Welcome Spring (p.3), published by Stacey in c.1925, was painted by Percy Tarrant, Margaret's father. He was a successful illustrator of magazines including *The Illustrated London News*, Cassell's *Family Magazine* and *The Girls' Own Paper*, and also of books and greeting cards. He encouraged Margaret to draw and paint. She used to enjoy playing at art shows, pinning her drawings in an 'Exhibition Tent' made from a clothes horse and dust sheets and inviting her parents inside to view the exhibits.

Drawing Room Tea, one of Miss Tarrant's illustrations in *Nursery Times and Playtime Rhymes* by Harry Golding, Ward Lock, 1923. Alas, the small boy does not seem to be enjoying his visit!

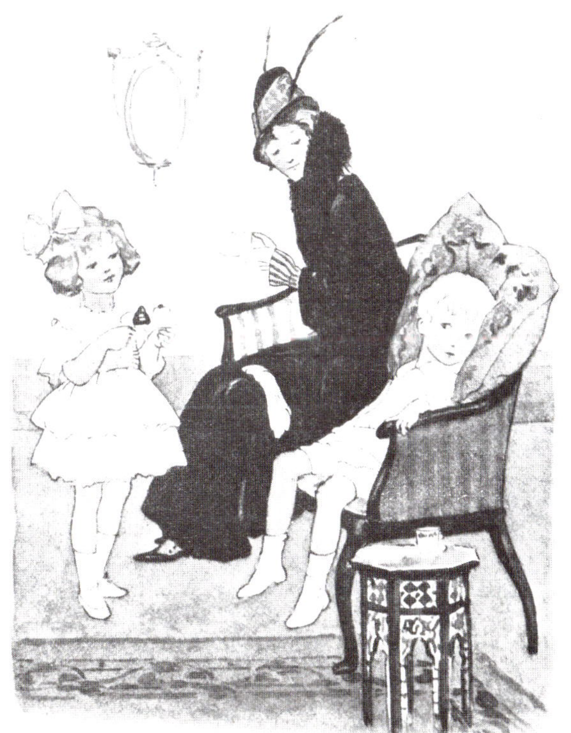

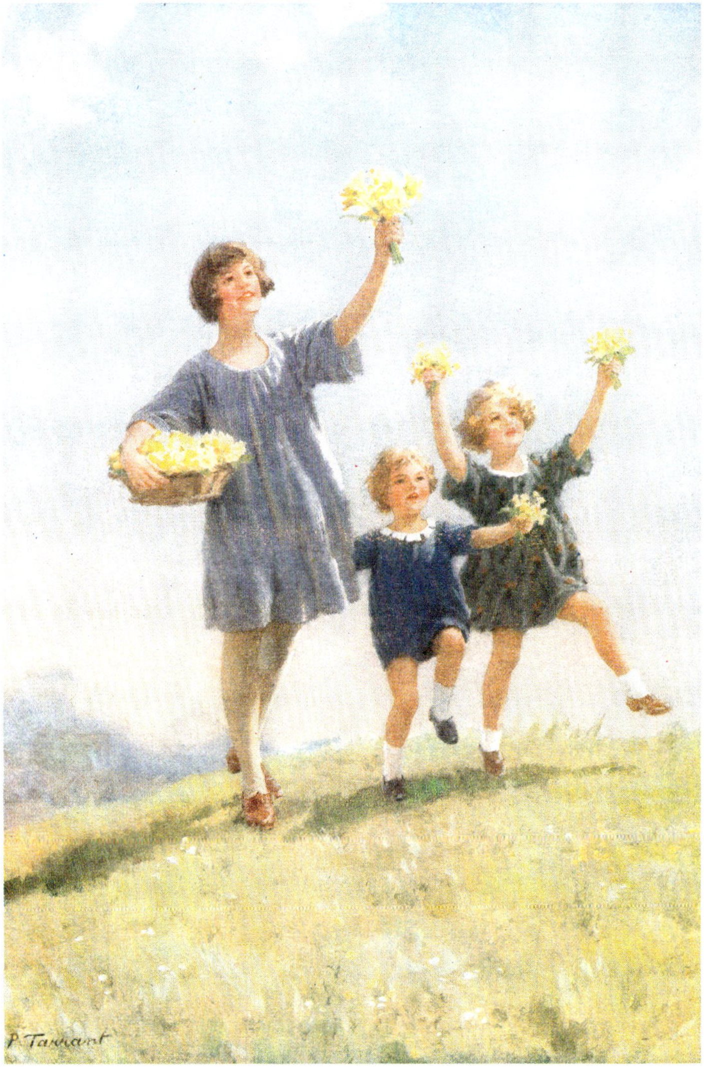

Welcome Spring by Percy Tarrant. c.1925.

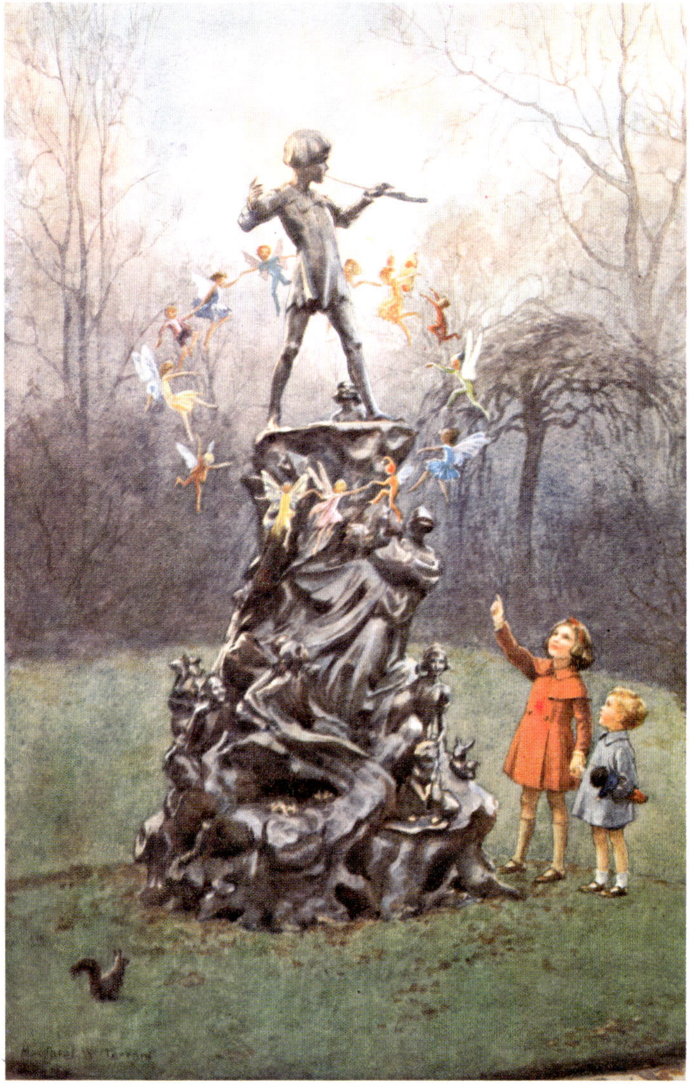

Peter's Friends. 1921.

In 1920 Margaret Tarrant started work on a series of imaginative pictures for the Medici Society. **Peter's Friends,** published in 1921, shows Sir George Frampton's well-known statue erected in Kensington Gardens in 1912 with two children gazing wistfully at it and many fairies dancing round it. Sir James Barrie's books on Peter Pan including *Peter Pan in Kensington Gardens,* 1906, *Peter and Wendy,* 1911, and the play of 1904 are all about the boy who wouldn't grow up. Peter took the Darling family – Wendy, John, and Michael – to all the excitement of Never-never land where they met Redskins and Pirates, the terrifying Captain Hook, the crocodile and the kindly Smee. Peter also had adventures in Kensington Gardens. The books and the play were much loved by children and grown ups and this picture was reproduced over and over again by the Medici Society.

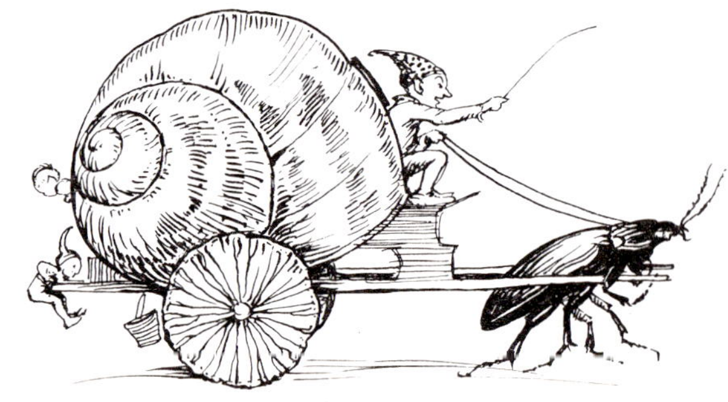

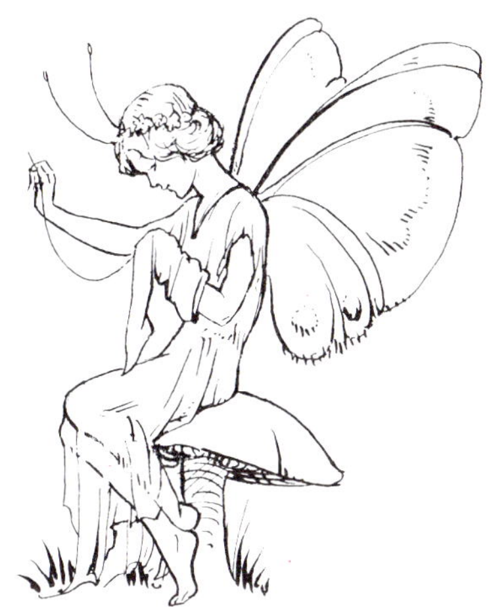

Do You Believe in Fairies? 1922.

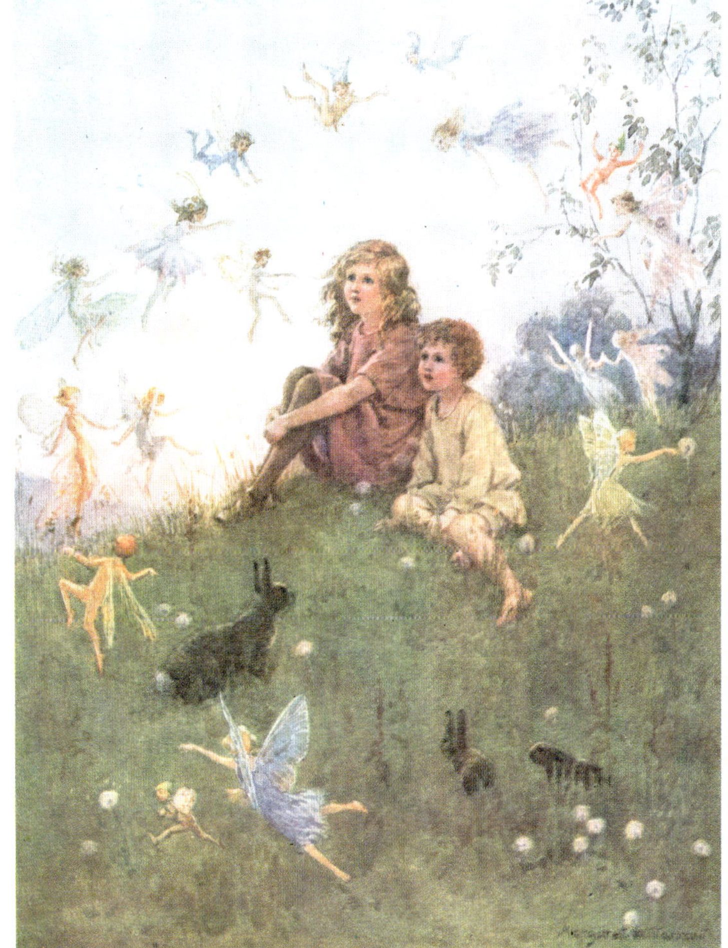

Do you believe in Fairies? published in 1922 also shows two children gazing at a ring of fairies as they dance round in the air. 1922 was the year that Sir Arthur Conan Doyle published his book *The Coming of the Fairies,* which included reproductions of photographs of fairies said to have been taken by two young and innocent girls at Cottingley near Bradford in Yorkshire. Sir Arthur is especially remembered for his book *The Adventures of Sherlock Holmes,* published in 1891, and for other books dealing with the fascinating and often blood-curdling adventures of the detective and his friend Dr Watson.

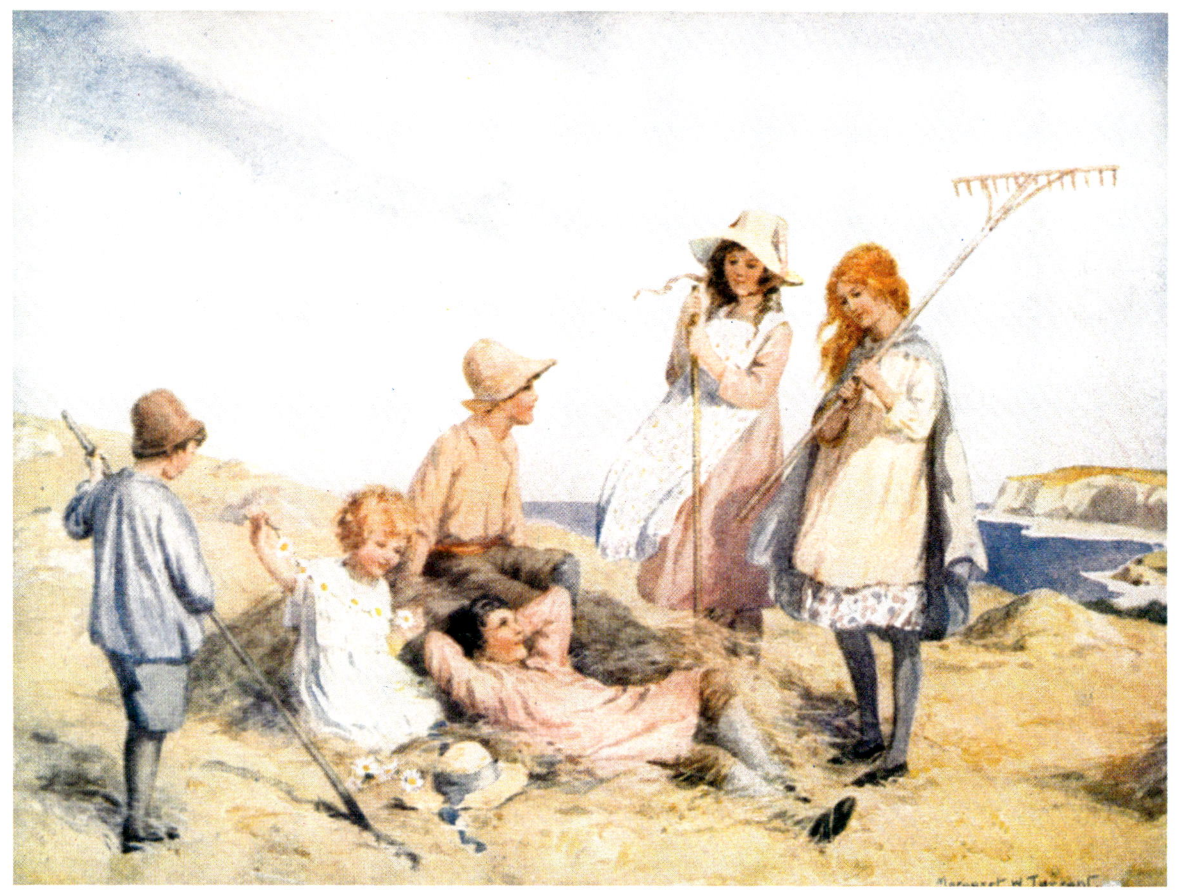

The Haymakers was published in 1923. It shows Margaret Tarrant's typical happy faces of childhood

Wherever she went, Margaret Tarrant was perpetually sketching and drawing, often with feverish activity. She used her friends and neighbours as models for her drawings. One neighbour remembers lying hunched on Miss Tarrant's floor in the role of a dying pirate, and visitors to the house would often be asked literally to 'lend a hand' while Margaret or her father drew it.

But Margaret Tarrant's main interest was in children. A neighbour describes how her baby daughter was drawn. Miss Tarrant would start a number of sketches, moving from one to another as the child changed position. 'I remember particularly a page of arms and hands and a baby fist clutching a bar of the play pen'. With older children she was able to concentrate on one or two more finished sketches. She would then invent her composition, adapting the figures which were seldom individual portraits and place them in imaginary settings, perhaps using sketches she had made on a holiday abroad or in the Surrey countryside.

The Snow Flake Fairies was one of the illustrations for *The Weather Fairies* by Marion St.John Webb, published by the Medici Society in 1925. It is interesting to see that the fairies are dressed in contemporary children's clothes of the period.

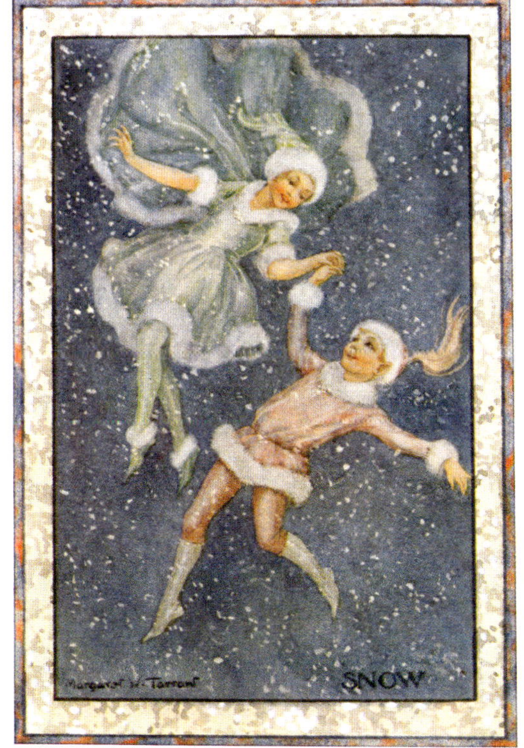

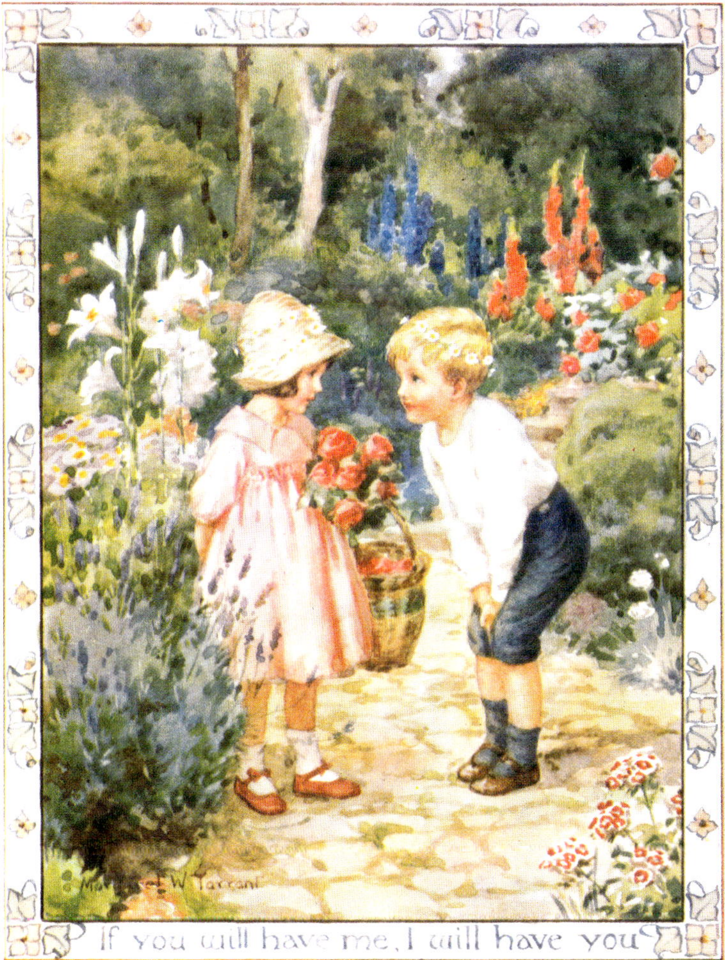

If you will have me, I will have you. Perhaps Miss Tarrant had the idea of a possible card for St. Valentine's day (February 14th) in mind when she thought up this attractive and appealing picture.

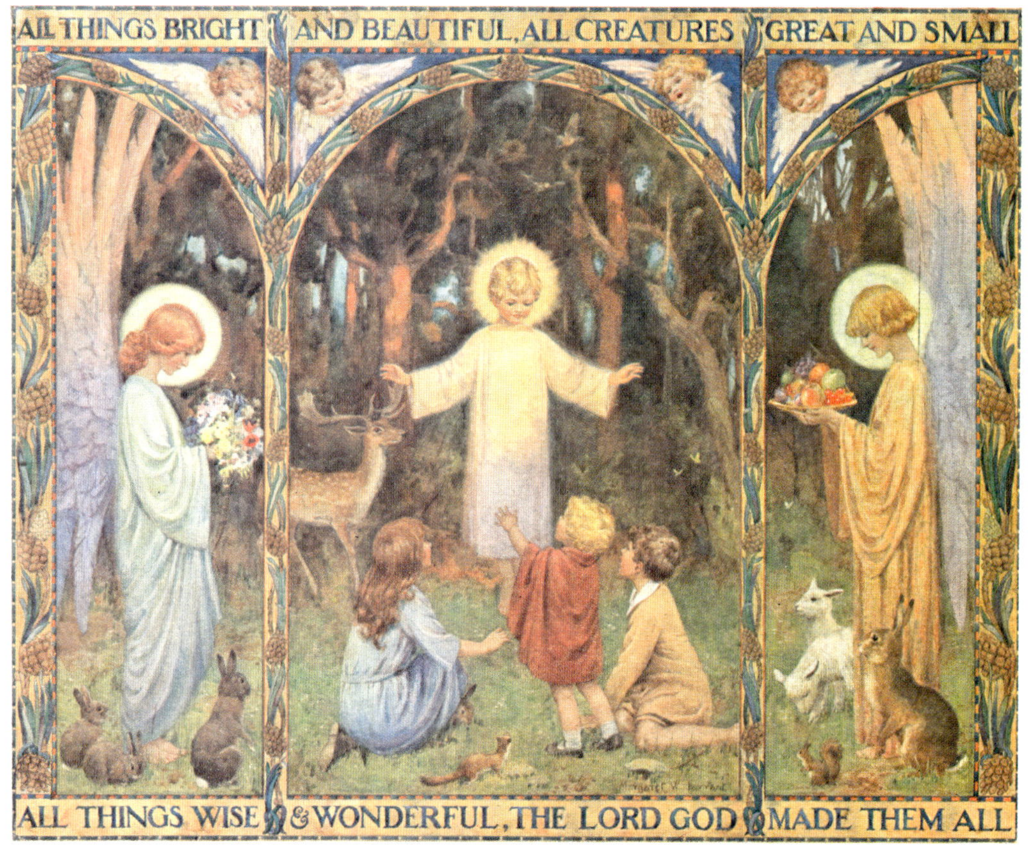

All Things Wise and Wonderful was first published in 1925 and proved to be the most popular of all Margaret Tarrant's paintings. In the period of the Great Slump around the year 1930, when trade was difficult, some art dealers were reported to have been able to keep their shops going thanks to the sale of framed copies of this much sought-after picture. It illustrates the first verse of the very popular hymn 'All Things Bright and Beautiful' by the renowned hymn writer Mrs Alexander (1818-1895). She was the wife of the Archbishop of Armagh. 'Once in Royal David's City,' the Christmas hymn, was also written by Mrs Alexander.

The decorative border of pine cones divides the picture into three, like an altar-piece. The glowing colours and wealth of detail down to toadstools, daisies and butterflies captured the

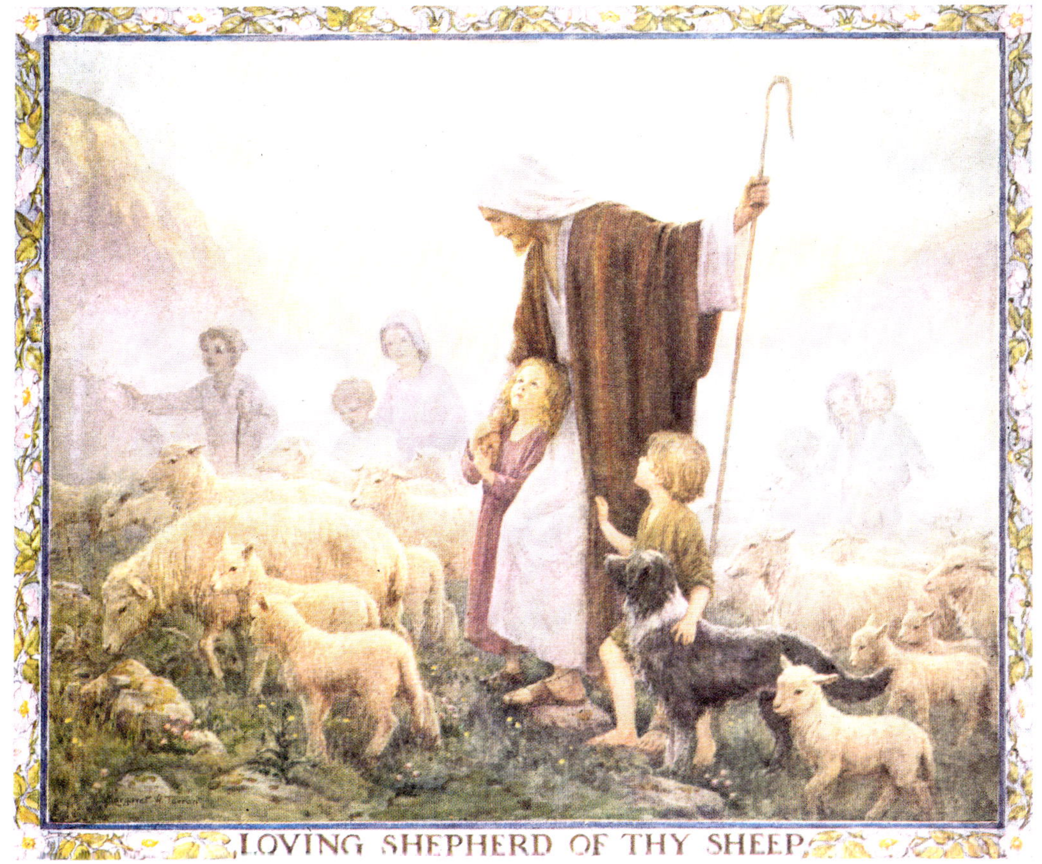

children's imagination. The success of **All Things** lead to the painting of a companion picture, **The Star of Bethlehem,** with wording 'The Dayspring from on high hath visited us' as in St. Luke's Gospel, chapter 1, verse 78. This was published in 1926 and also proved very popular.

Loving Shepherd, another of Miss Tarrant's religious pictures, published in 1927, is based on Jesus' reference to himself as the Good Shepherd.

Margaret Tarrant was deeply religious and much of her life centred on the activities of the parish church. She was active in arranging sales of work for the Church Missionary Society, helped decorate the church for festivals and at one time acted as car provider and driver for the vicar who had no car of his own.

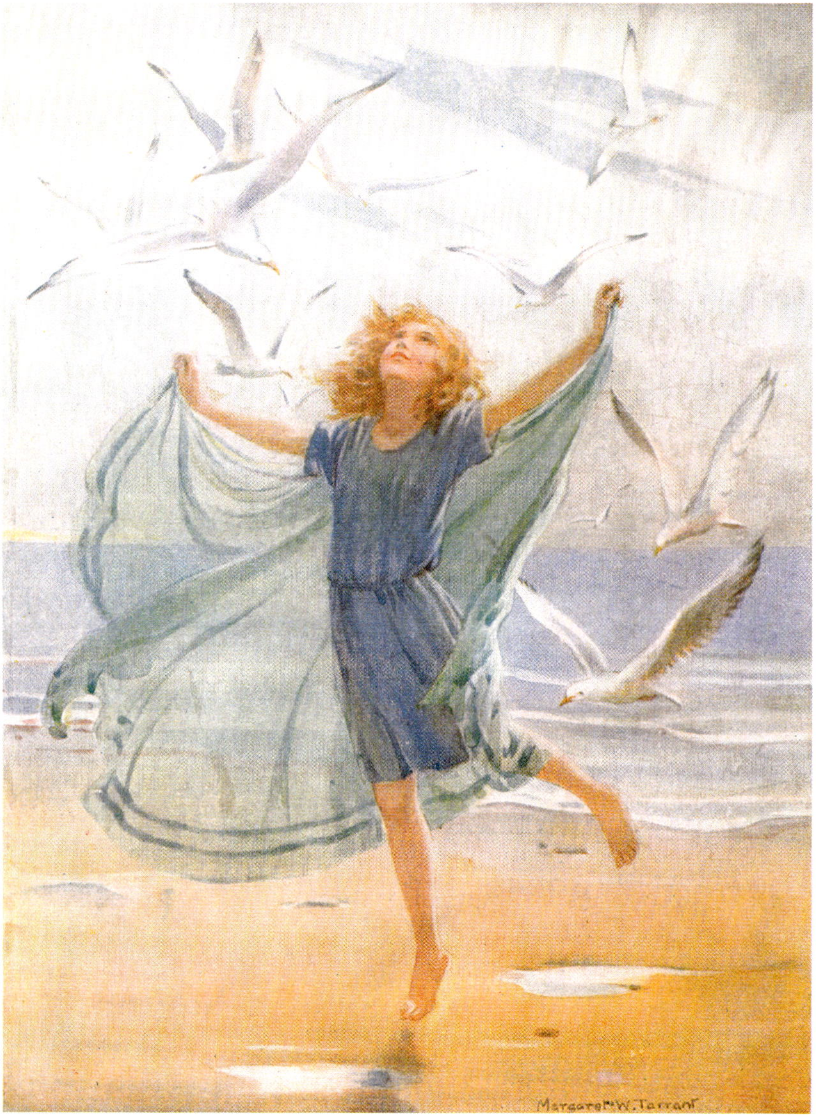

Sea Joy was published in 1926. See also the picture on the front cover published in 1922. Both are inspired by the dancing of Isadora Duncan (1878-1927), the United States dancer. She based her dance movements on natural happenings such as the rhythmic movement of the waves of the sea. She toured Europe and America giving exhibitions of her

Sea Joy. 1926.

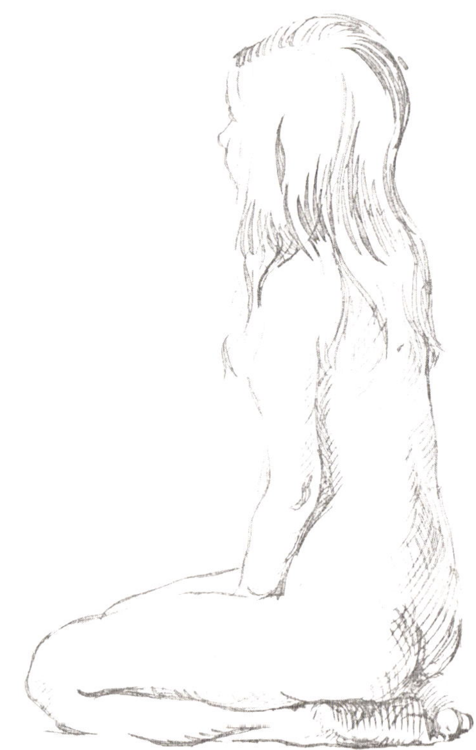

Sketch of kneeling girl. 1916.

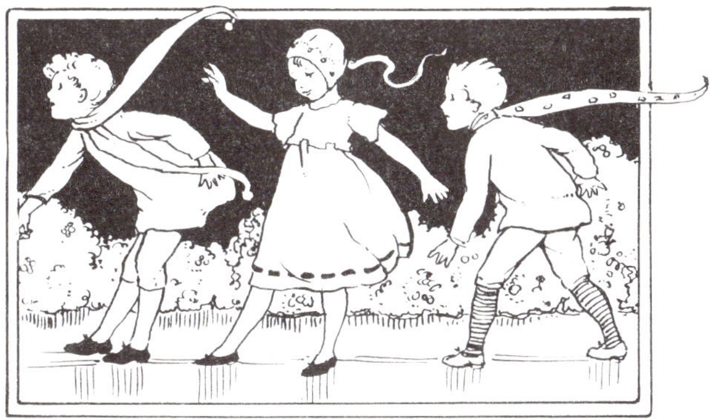

dancing. Wearing a loose tunic she danced barefoot, as suggested by Greek sculptures. One can imagine Miss Tarrant's eagerness and enthusiasm as she sat in the theatre watching Isadora's every movement through her black and gold opera glasses and memorising this for future paintings. There was great tragedy in Isadora's life as her children were drowned in Versailles and she herself was accidentally killed in Nice.

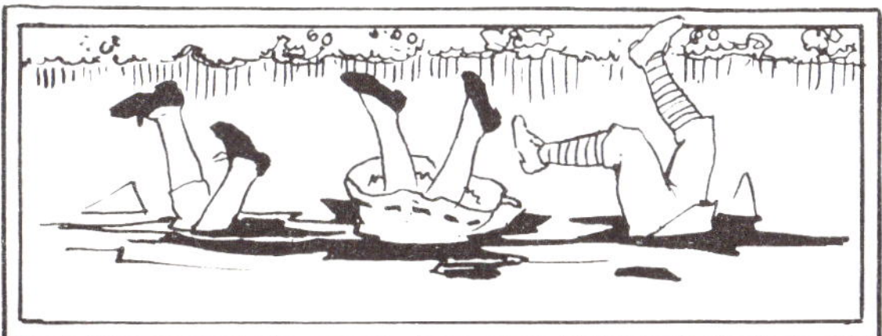

Bringing Home the Holly and Mistletoe. This design was one of a number of Christmas card pictures which Miss Tarrant produced for the Medici in 1927 when the Society was expanding its selection of greeting cards. The Medici Society had first published Christmas cards about the year 1914 and pioneered the idea of offering these with reproductions of Old Master and Modern paintings which did not include holly, snow scenes and the like. Other 1927 designs by Miss Tarrant included a scene of a choir of angels, children carol singing, and the three kings in the stable at Bethlehem. Each picture is painted in a circle with an elaborate border design — compare with the borders of the pictures on pp. 7-8. Many of these cards were sold in America.

Bringing Home the Holly and Mistletoe. 1927.

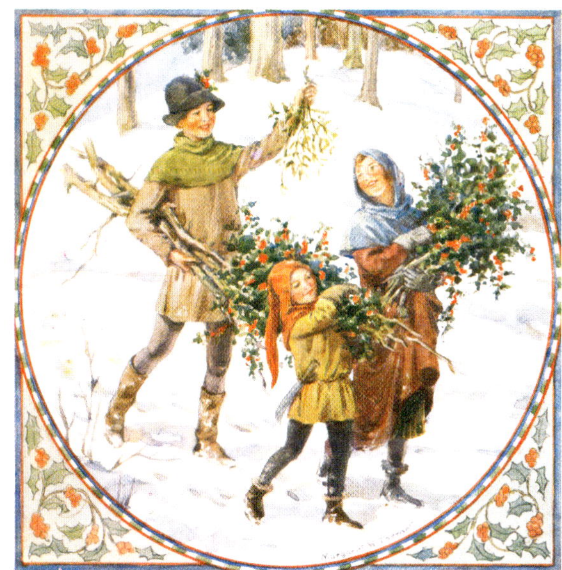

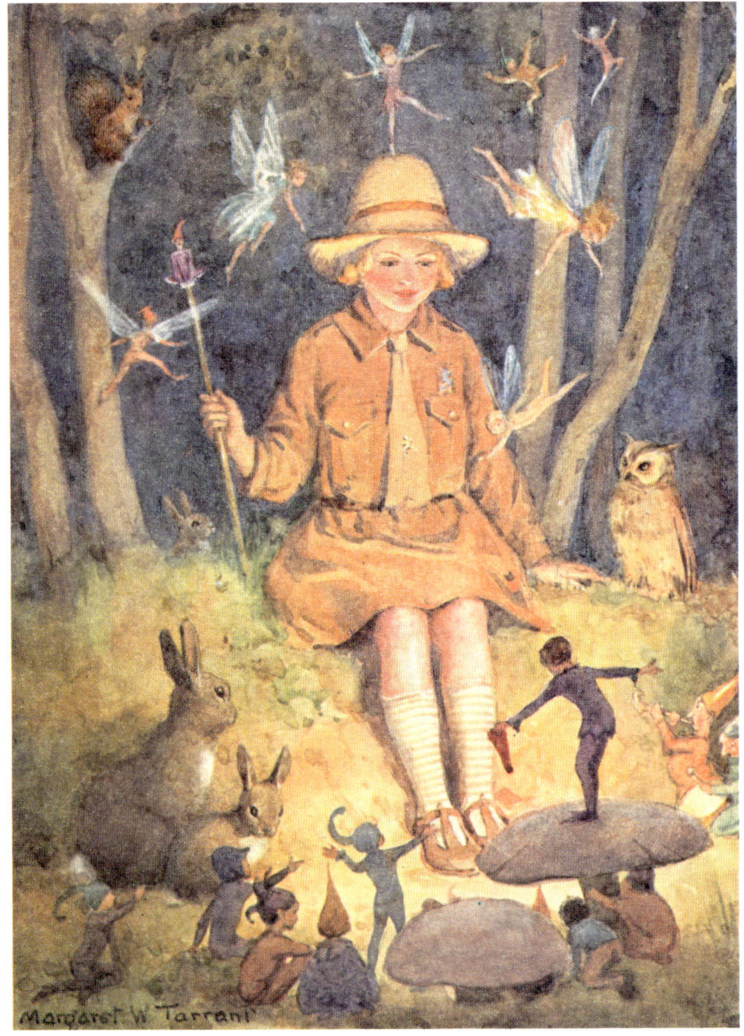

Queen of the Brownies was a 1926 design showing a fanciful picture of a Brownie with fairies (Brownie was the name given to younger Girl Guides aged from 7½ to 11. They wore brown uniforms as in this picture).

Margaret Tarrant designed many cards for the Girl Guide Movement.

The Girl Guides had been founded in 1910 by Lord Baden Powell and developed very quickly both in the British Isles and overseas. Soon there were hundreds of thousands of Guides in Great Britain alone.

Lord Baden Powell was a distinguished General in the British Army who had been especially interested in sending out scouts to find out what the enemy were doing, and in 1899 had written a book on scouting for the army. In 1907, feeling that young people would enjoy the idea of scouting, he organised a camp of 21 boys on Brownsea Island in Poole Harbour. This was a great success and the Scout Movement was founded in the following year. Scouts had to make a promise to be loyal, helpful to others, trustworthy, friendly and considerate to all Scouts, courageous, and to make good use of their time. Special emphasis was laid on learning useful crafts and learning about natural history and the like.

The Guide Movement was founded on the same lines as the Boy Scouts with training in good citizenship etc. Lady Baden Powell was for years their leader. All this fitted in admirably with Miss Tarrant's kindly and loving nature and her joy in painting pictures of the countryside.

Girl Guide Camp, painted in 1929, shows Guides bringing firewood for their camp fire.

Cooking the Stew for lunch, another picture painted by Miss Tarrant for cards for Guides to send. Alas, the big wood fire with great pot balanced on it looks very dangerous.

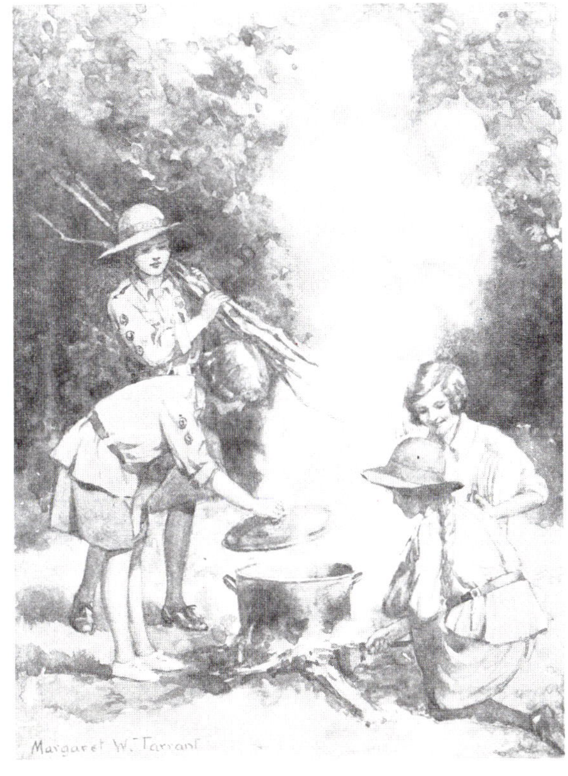

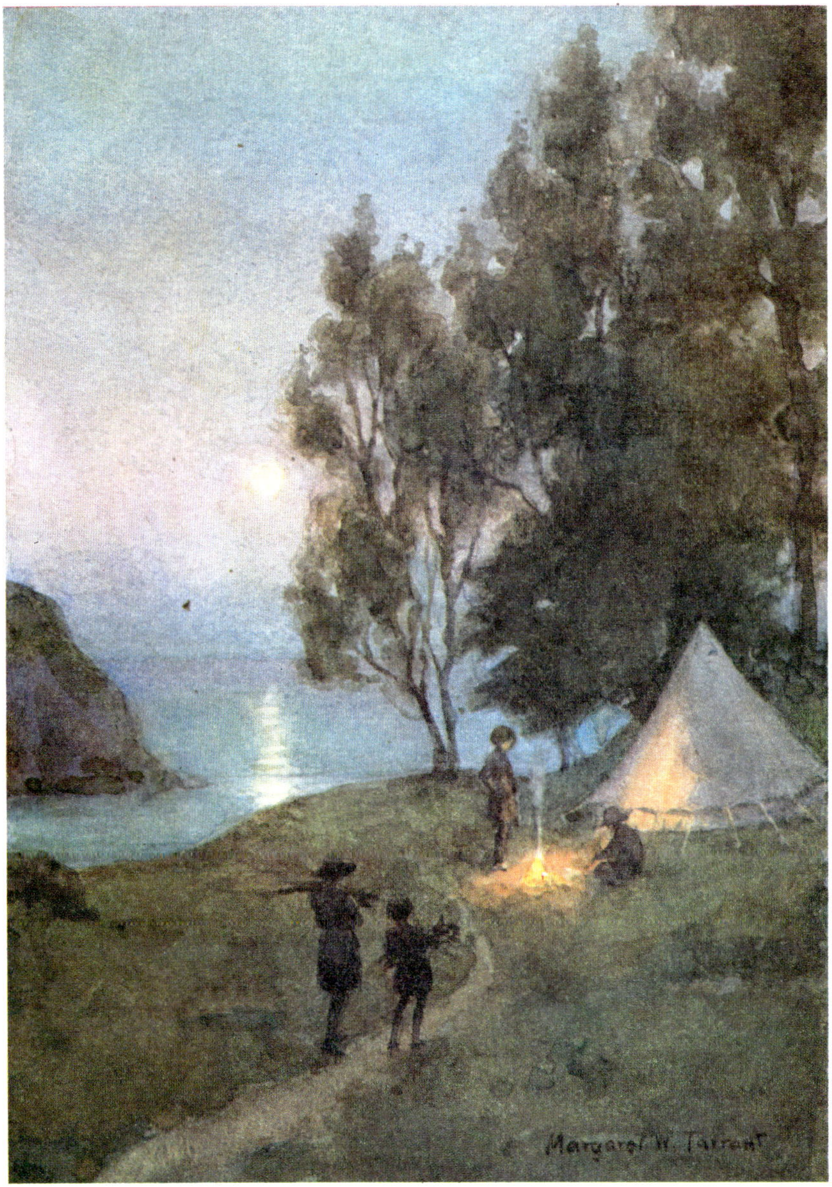

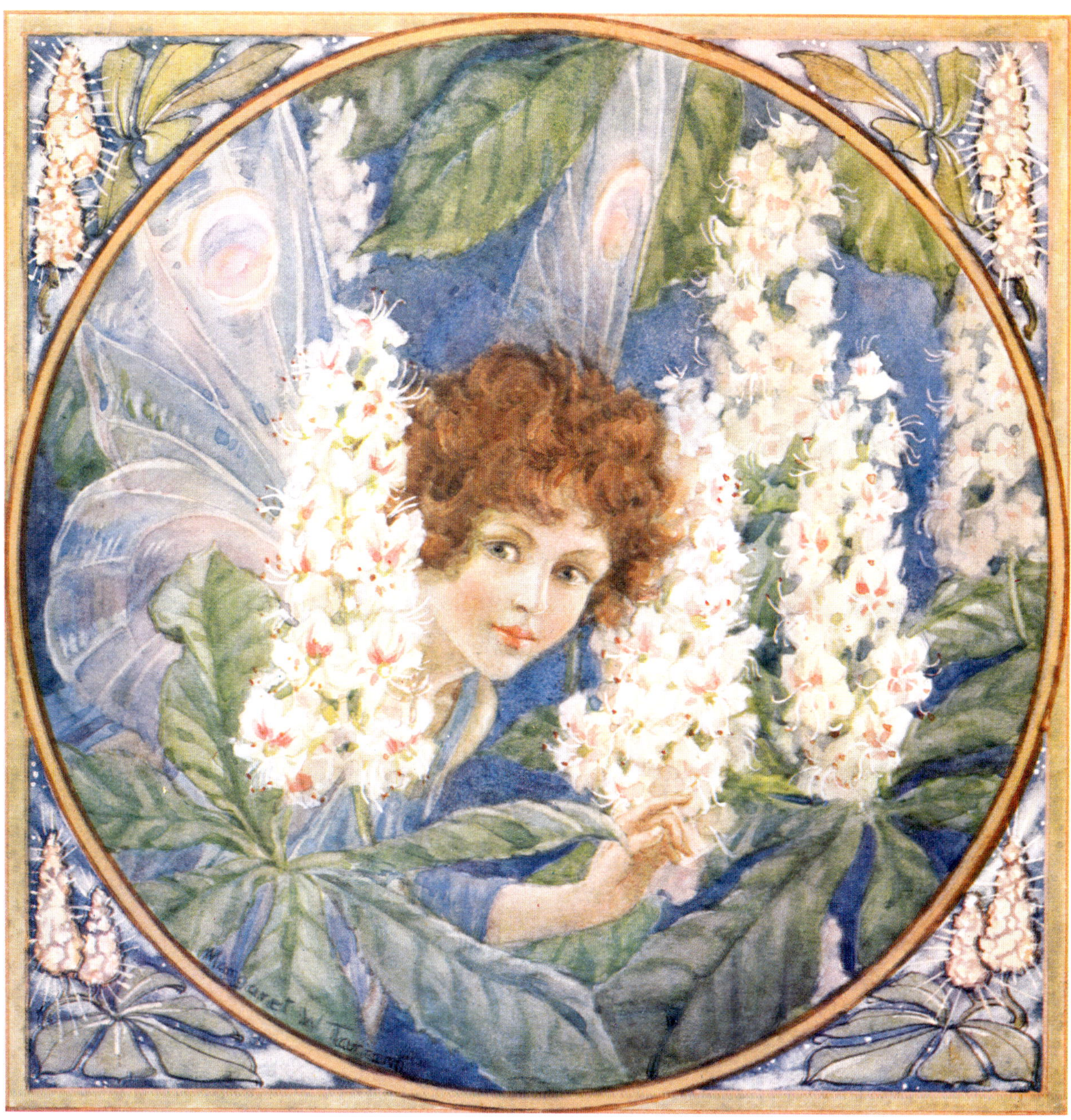

Chestnut Candles. 1928.

Chestnut Candles painted in 1928 although a comparatively simple composition is full of interest and charm with the attractive red-haired fairy and the magnificent horse chestnut flowers with their promise of 'conkers' in the autumn — so beloved by children. Note the circular design and border, with its decorations, which is typical of much of her work at this period — compare with the pictures on pp. 8 and 11.

Margaret Tarrant constantly painted pictures of fairies. In 1909, when she was 21, her first series of fairy postcards was published by C. W. Faulkner & Co.. See also p. 2, for the series of fairy subjects painted for George G. Harrap & Co. and later for the Medici Society.

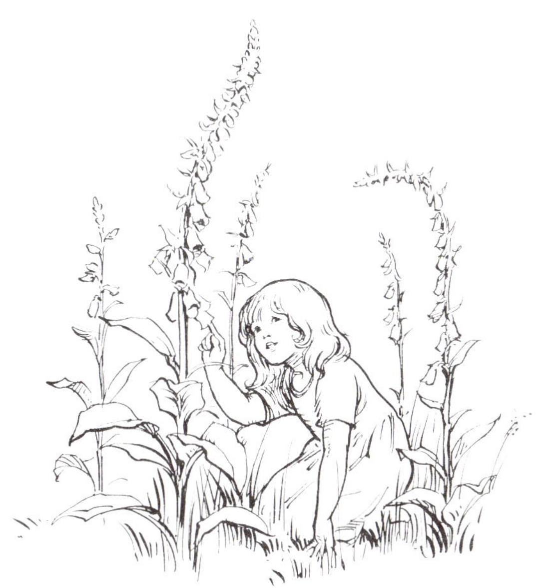

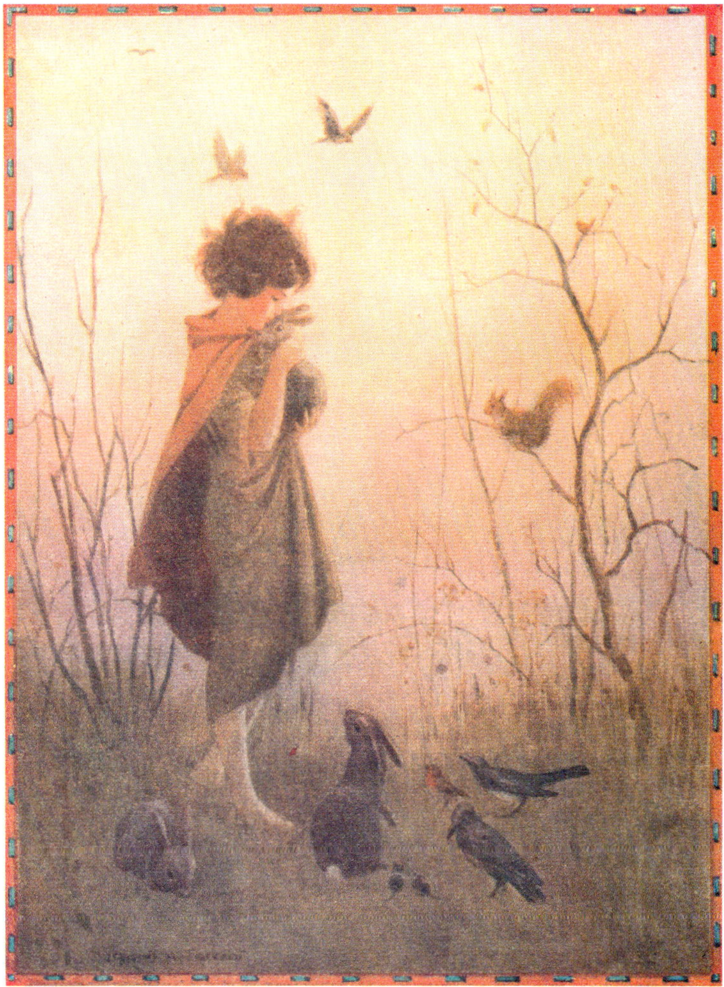

Woodland Friends painted in 1930 again shows Margaret Tarrant's love of nature. It was a joy to her to walk in the countryside and she had a great knowledge of wild flowers, birds and animals. She was always very meticulous in her observation so that she could make sure that she drew everything correctly.

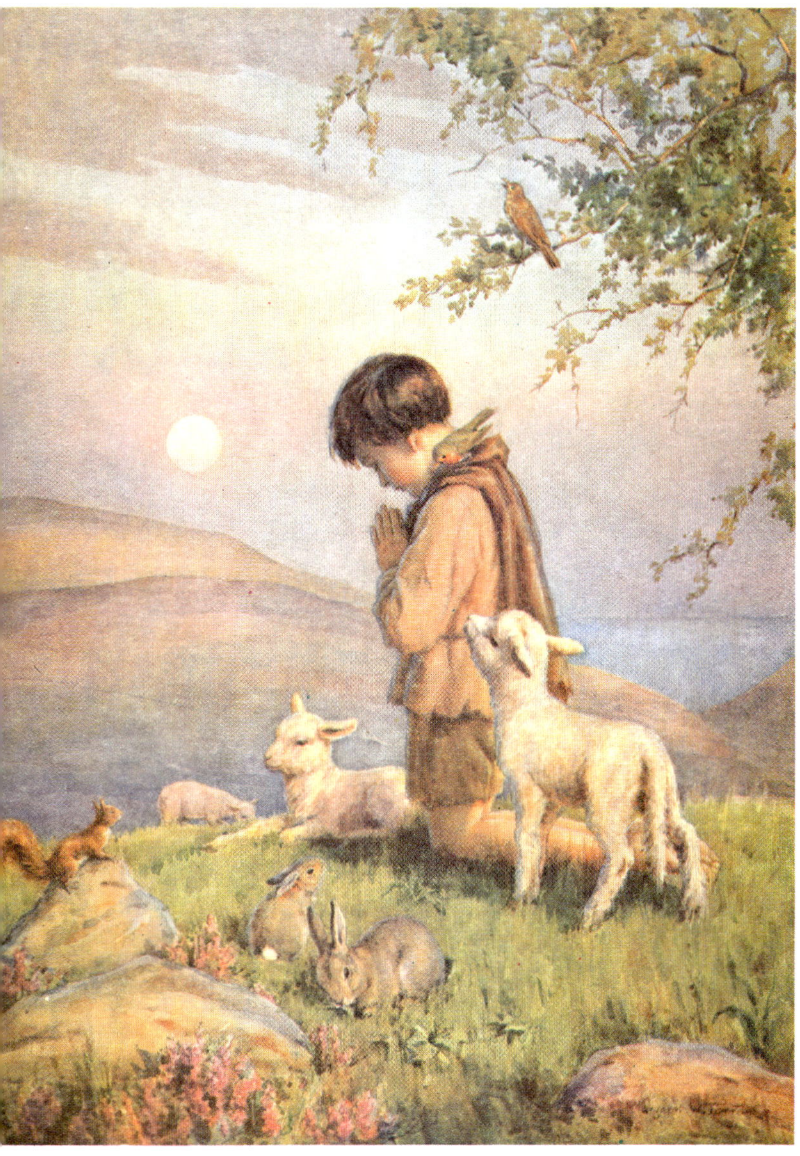

He Prayeth Best. 1933.

He Prayeth Best who loveth Best
All things both great and small;
For the dear God who loveth us,
He made and loveth all.
S. T. Coleridge

He Prayeth Best derives its title from the final lines of 'The Rhyme of the Ancient Mariner' by the poet Samuel Coleridge (1772-1834) — a great friend of Wordsworth. It was a very sad period in Margaret Tarrant's life. She was now 45 and for the last three years had been nursing and supporting her parents who were now far from well. Her father had been losing his sight and needed her help to finish off the fine detail on his paintings. She must have had little time and energy to do her own painting and drawing. Though she enjoyed cooking and jam making, life must have been hard at times. One can imagine her often praying, like the boy in the picture, when things were most difficult. Perhaps this gave her the idea for the scene. In 1934 both her parents died — within three months of each other. She had written to the Medici Society during her father's final illness 'I miss his ever ready criticism and help with my work so much . . . I may say that I have no other relatives.'

She was not finding it easy to think out new ideas for her pictures, so in 1936 the Medici Society paid for her to spend six weeks in Palestine to see the land where Jesus had lived and to sketch native costumes and buildings. It was hoped that this would give her a real break and holiday and perhaps inspire her to produce further religious paintings — though perhaps of a rather different character from those she had previously painted.

Miss Tarrant seems to have been thrilled with what she saw in Palestine and to have sketched very hard and enthusiastically painting and drawing what she saw, including many attractive views of places mentioned in the Gospels such as Jerusalem, Nazareth, the Sea of Galilee and Bethlehem. She frequently wrote to her friend and fellow artist, Cecily Mary Barker (1895-

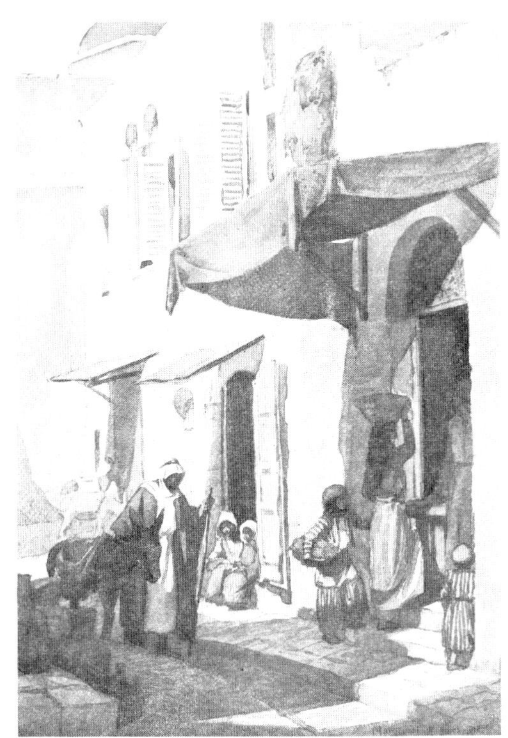

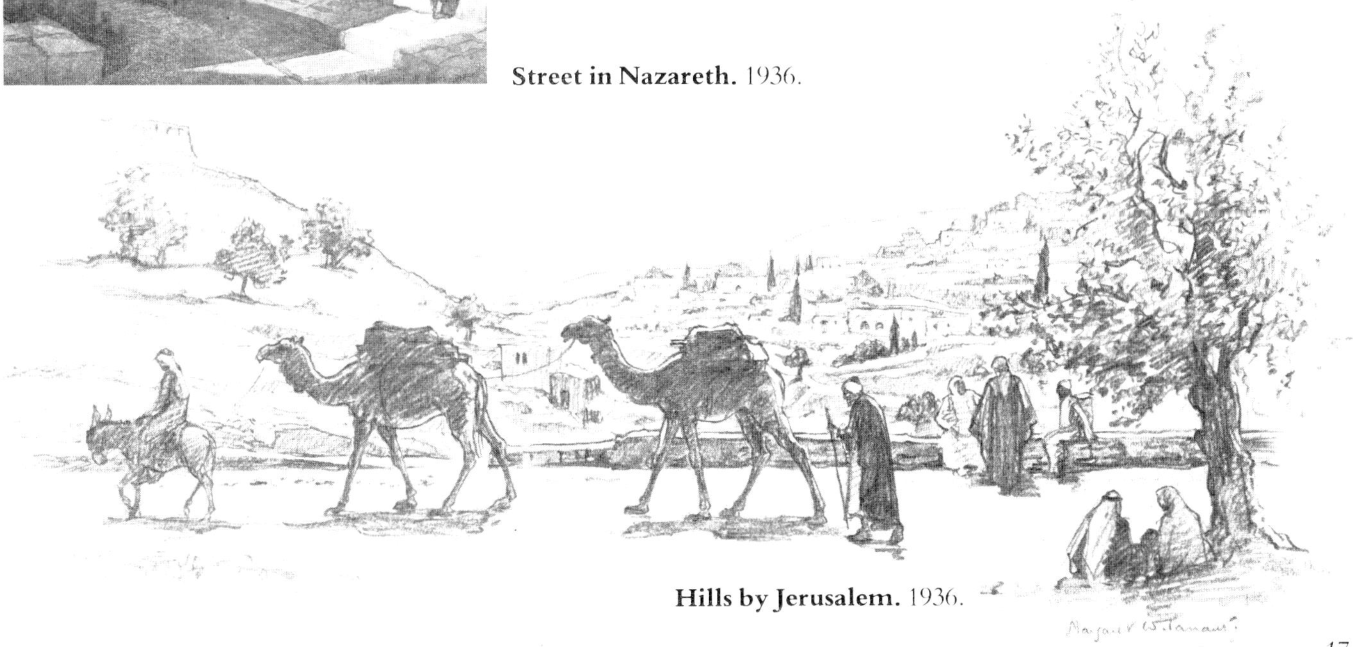

Street in Nazareth. 1936.

Hills by Jerusalem. 1936.

1973). She was evidently awed by what she saw and this made her critical of her earlier imaginatve religious pictures. She felt that she must penetrate to the spiritual aspects of her travels, realising 'that this is the country where Christ lived'.

She describes the sunsets: wonderful electric blue in the folds and gullies of the Moab hills; pink, nearly crimson, of the Sea of Galilee; the drive from Jerusalem to Nazareth 'extraordinary country ... doing wonderful serpentine curves up and downhill ... with people working in the fields in indescribably vivid colours — wild orange, yellow, crimson, scarlet and magenta ....' She made many paintings of the people seen in the various towns 'so much native costume among the modernity'. The Bedouin children would

The Sea of Galilee, 1936. What a lot of Gospel stories this picture conjures up.

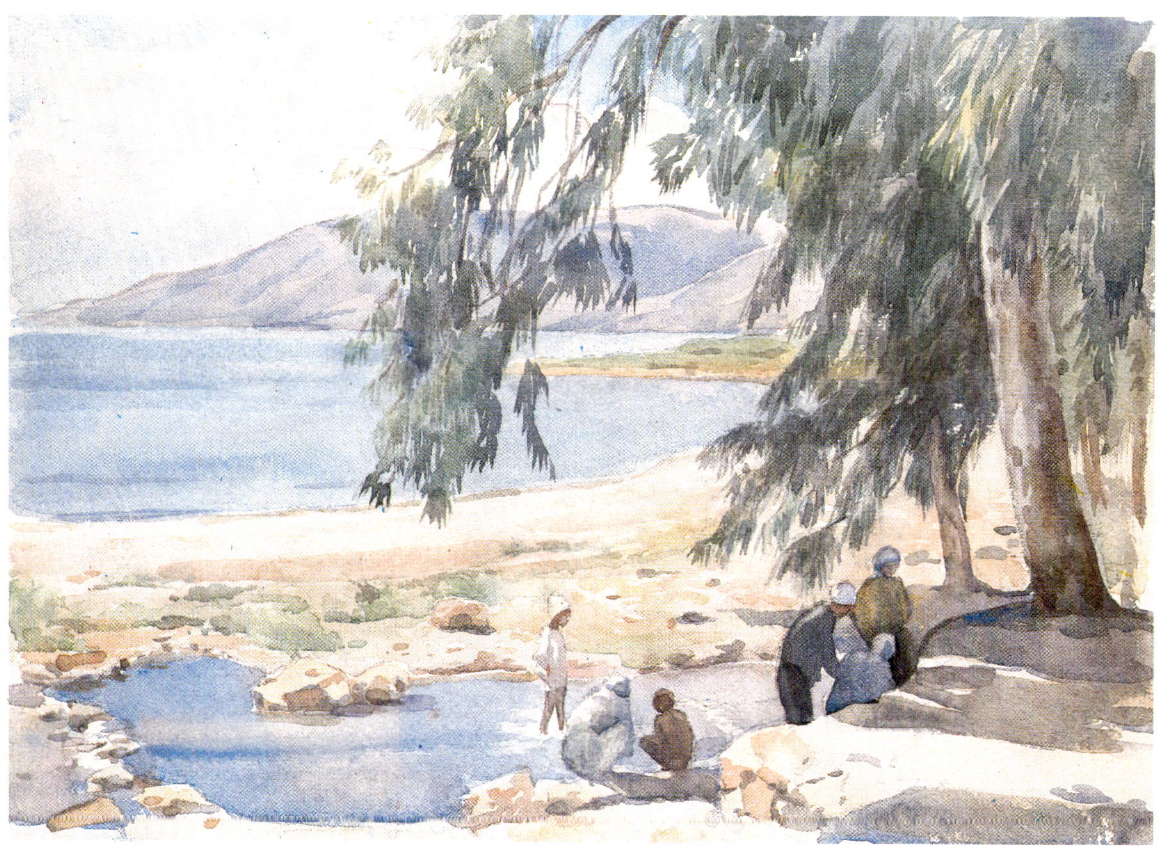

Sketches from Miss Tarrant's Palestine Sketchbook.

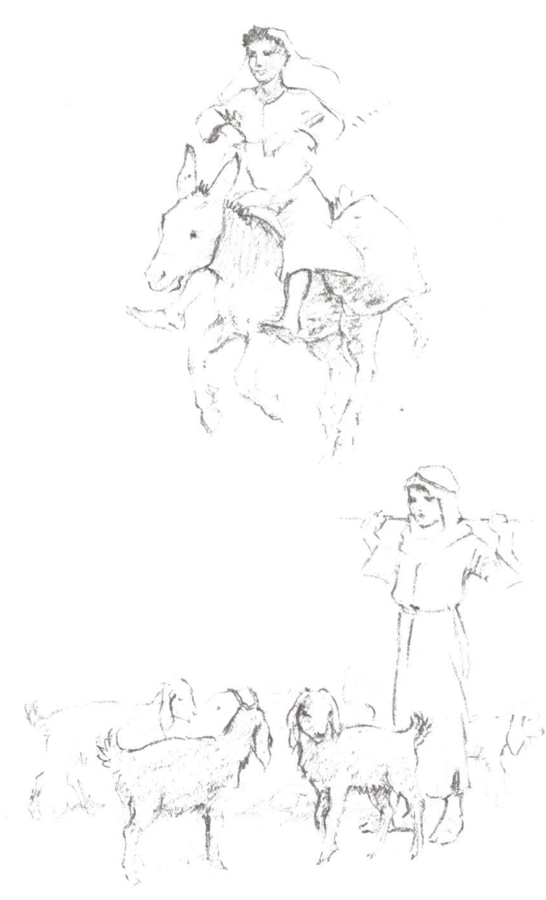

pester her to buy shell necklaces and give 'back-sheesh' 'but if you laugh at them and tease them they soon give up and laugh too, and the ones whom I have photo'd and sketched remember and greet me with joyful grins, and occasionally kiss my hand'.

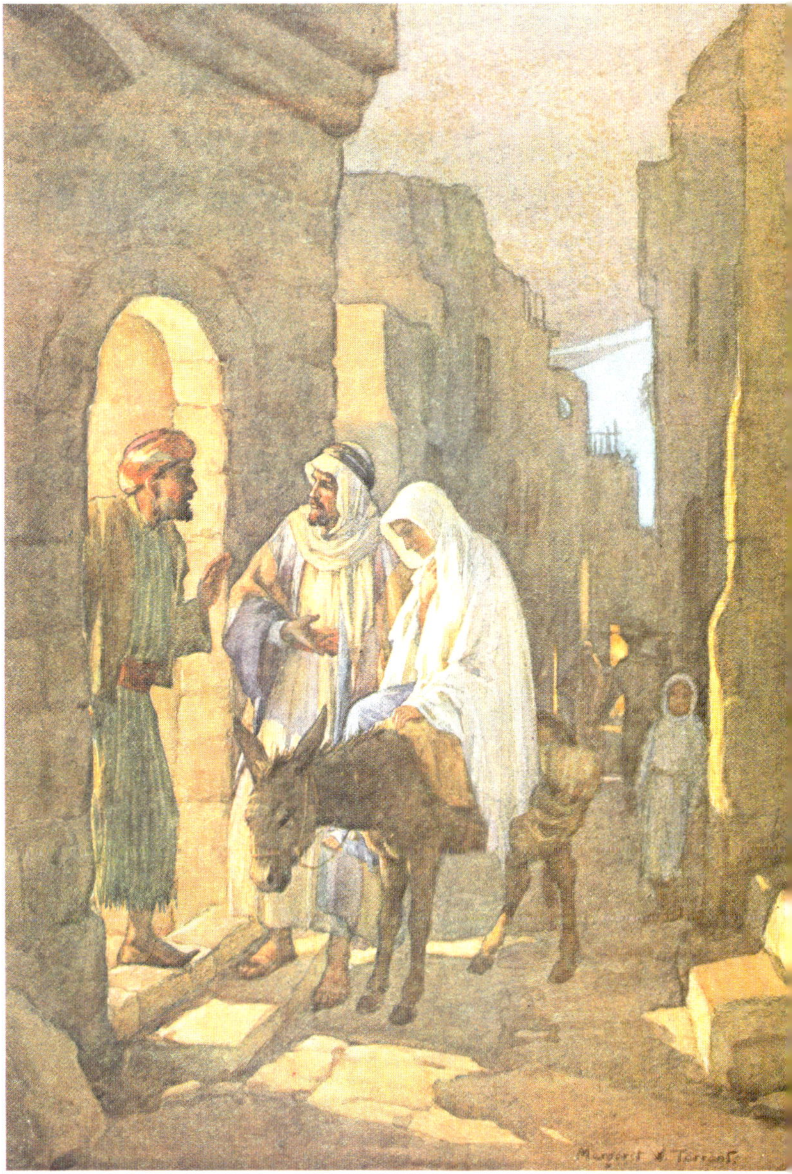

No Room at the Inn. c.1938.

Britain's Treasure. 1939.

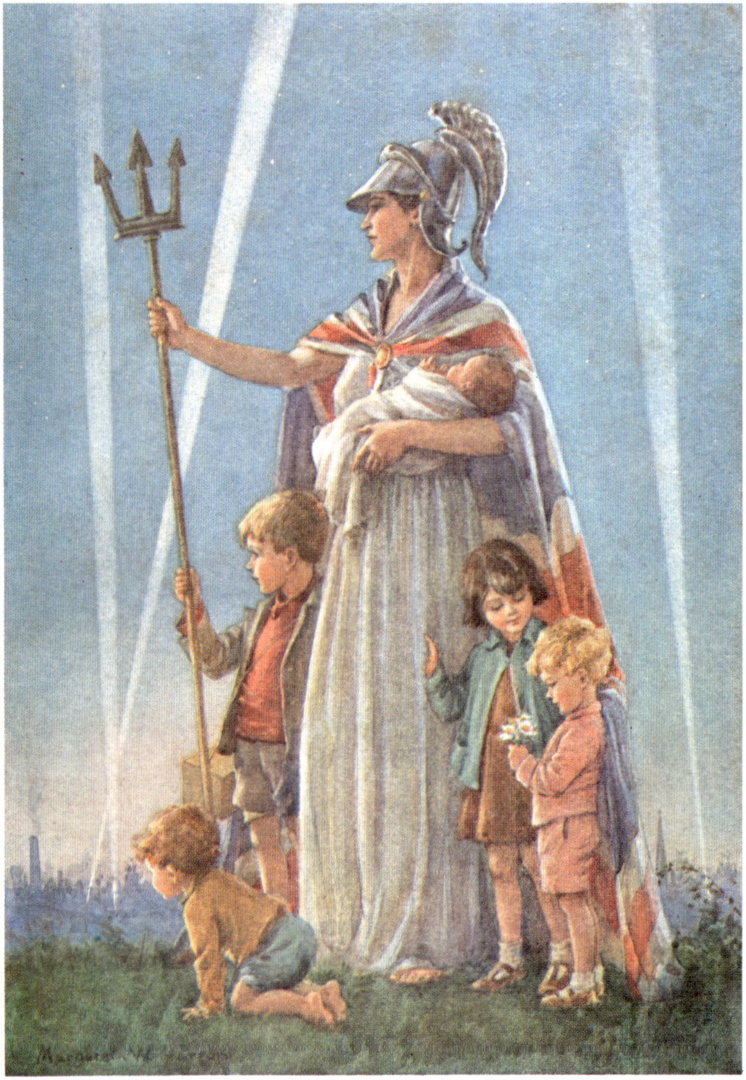

When the 1939-1945 war broke out many town children were evacuated to houses in the country for fear that the Germans would carry out devastating air raids on London and other major towns. Miss Tarrant painted a number of pictures as 'a small contribution to help and cheer one or two people at this time'. One of these, **Britain's Treasure,** shows the figure of Britannia wearing her helmet and carrying her trident with five children who look calm and safe, while in the distance searchlights scour the sky for bombing planes. She also designed a series of postcards showing typical scenes of farm life for the many children evacuated to the country.

From 1936 onwards Margaret Tarrant produced many paintings of wild flowers growing in their natural surroundings for the Medici wild flower series of postcards. She took infinite

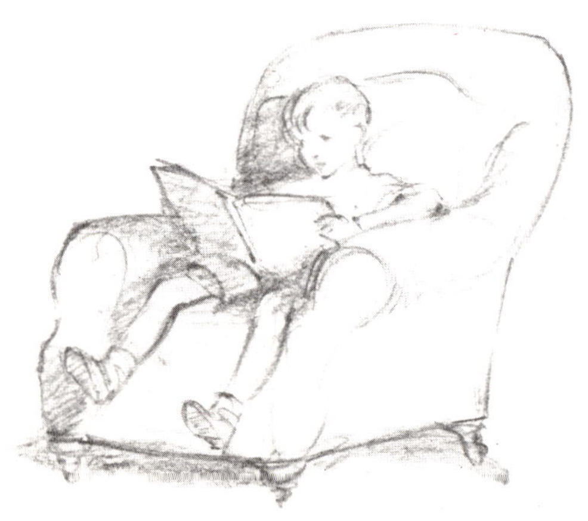

trouble in searching for plants to paint, sketching them partly on the spot and often taking photographs of them to help her to work on the picture at home and ensure that all details were accurate. Between 1937 and 1952 she contributed 63 subjects to this series which proved very popular. See illustration on p.22.

During these years Miss Tarrant also painted pictures for reproduction as large prints for children's rooms and schools. A typical example is **The Fairy Way,** published in 1942, showing an entrancing procession of a Queen of the fairies going along a woodland path, preceeded by her band and followed by her retinue stretching into the far distance. See also **Lesson Time** (p.23) with an elf giving a lesson to the animals and birds. She painted many other pictures of elves and animals: an elphin chorus, the race through

The Fairy Way. 1942.

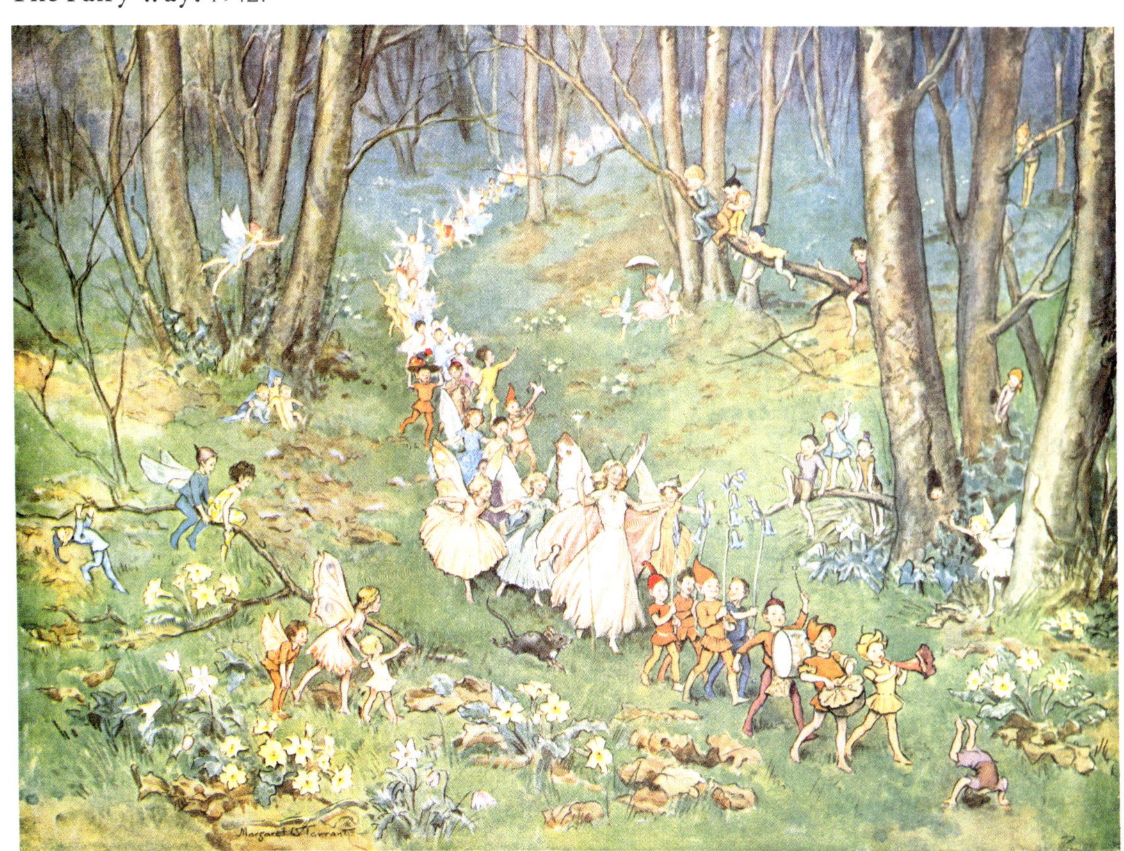

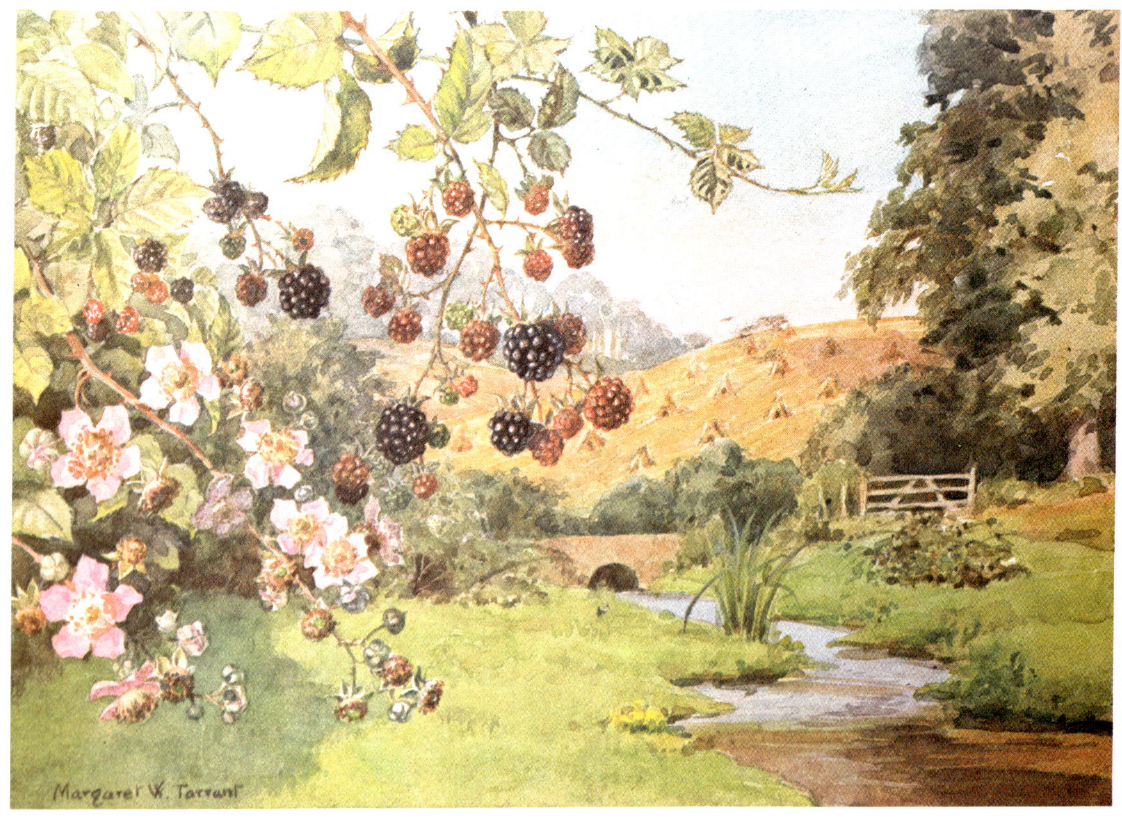

Blackberry. 1947. (See page 21.)

the snow with rabbits drawing a sledge guided by an elf, market day with elf and animals, an elf to tea, water sports, woodland hospital etc. Miss Tarrant was very keen to paint a picture of a **Woodland Hospital** — showing an elf doctor sounding the chest of a rabbit patient with much else going on. She pointed out that children would not think it too gloomy and would be encouraged to take their hospital treatment calmly. This idea had been suggested to her by a nurse on a children's ward.

During the war and after she often got about the village on an ancient 'bike' to save petrol. A neighbour recalls how one day in 1944 or 5 she had allowed her three-year-old daughter to draw on two large shed doors in their garden, as in war time paper was short. Miss Tarrant leapt off her bicycle and asked to join in. She soon covered the

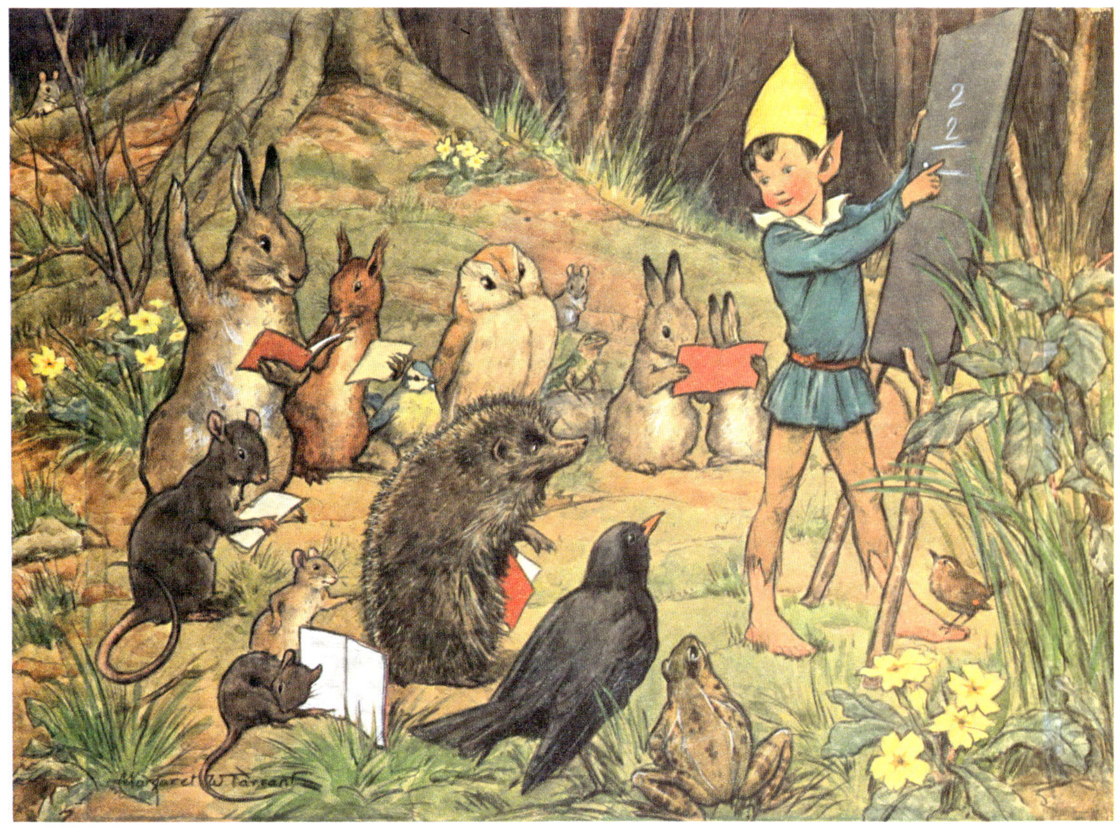

Lesson Time, 1945

two doors with a delightful array of rabbits, mice, fairies and lots of other creatures, and finished by saying, 'and here is Pamela!' — drawing the child herself in a lower right-hand corner. She then began to feel guilty about encouraging the child to draw on walls. The neighbour said that she was always full of energy and laughed easily. She had a heart complaint and her doctor told her to slow down but she could not remember to do so.

Woodland Hospital, 1949.

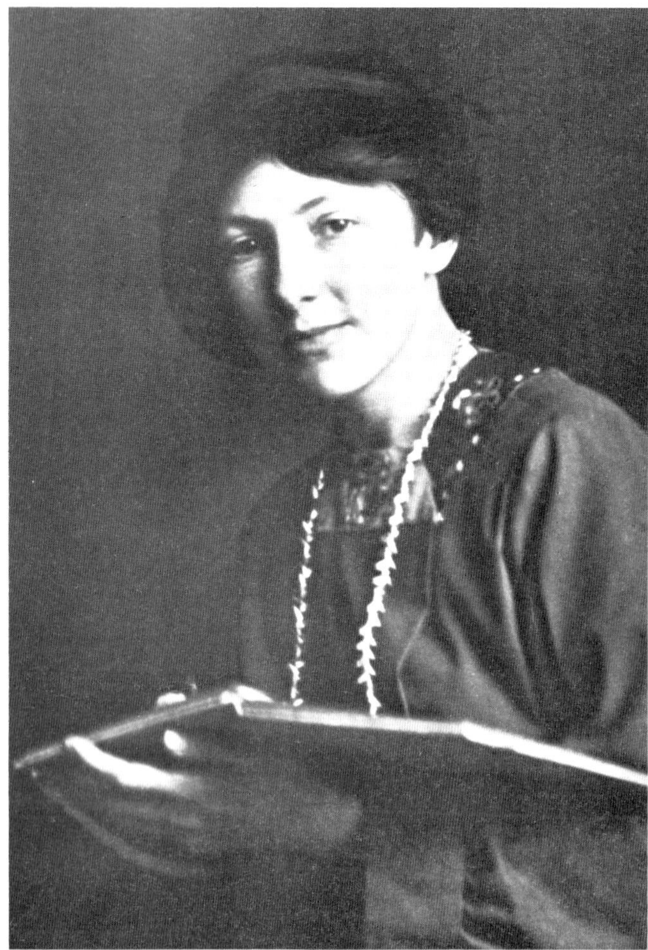

Margaret Tarrant in 1918.

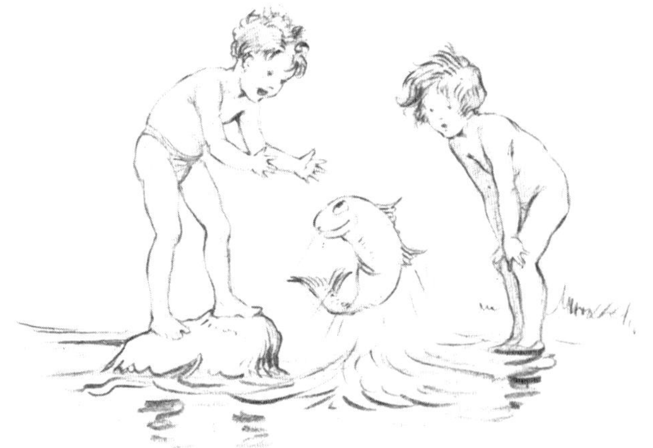

Margaret Tarrant giving a demonstration of painting to young admirers at the Peaslake Festival in 1949.

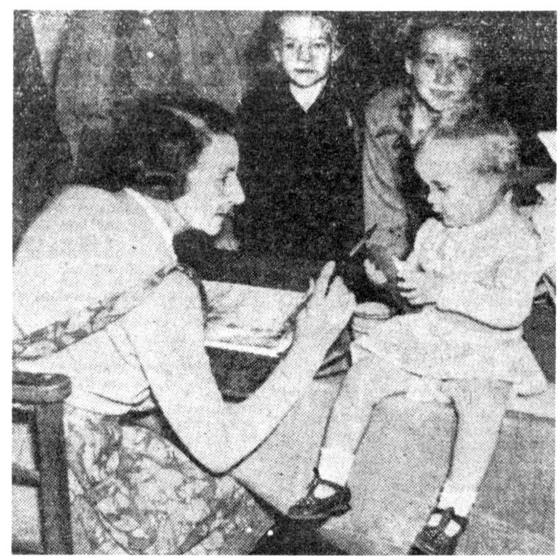

 ISBN 0 85503 063 1. First Published in 1982.